GIOVANNI CARANDENTE

Anthony Caro and Twentieth-Century Sculpture

MUSEUM WÜRTH
VERLAG PAUL SWIRIDOFF
1999

Foreword

FOR ME, AND FOR MANY OTHERS, the most important British sculptor since Henry Moore is Sir Anthony Caro. Several of his works are in the collection of the Museum Würth, the first having been acquired in 1995.

Today, Caro's sculpture is world famous and needs no further endorsement – especially not from a layman like me. However, I am again and again impressed how powerfully and directly the artist uses steel, stoneware and other materials, whilst at the same time imbuing his sculptures with a sense of lightness.

I met Anthony Caro for the first time in 1996 and we immediately took a great liking to each other. Time and again my observation about famous artists I have met was also true with Anthony Caro: modest, ingenious, charming and above all friendly with a sense of fun.

Reinhold Würth with Anthony Caro in his London studio discussing one of *The Last Judgement* sculptures, *Sacrifice*, July 1998

When I addressed him as Sir Anthony, in accordance with his title, he remarked that this honorary title is very nice and well meant, but that it is especially useful when making a reservation in a restaurant – for often he then gets a table at the window. So his good humour is not only written on his face and shows in his personality, but also in the character of his sculpture.

In 1998, together with my wife and the head of the museum, C. Sylvia Weber, I had the chance to visit Anthony Caro in his London studio, where he was busy working on parts of his *Last Judgement* sculpture. I was immediately intrigued. After having seen the model of the whole installation that he intended, I was moved and enthusiastic about the ambition, depth and scope of this work.

The Last Judgement will be shown to the public for the first time as part of the 1999 Venice Biennale. Without doubt it is one of the most important sculptures Anthony Caro has made: for in addition to its fine details, it expresses, with its challenging three-dimensionality, a depth of artistic creation that goes beyond the religious subject matter and will remain valid for all time.

Due to the current conflict in Kosovo – only a few flight minutes away from Venice – Caro's work has gained a dimension none of us could have foreseen. If there will ever be a Last Judgement or Divine Justice, these crimes will never be forgotten.

A work of art like this can only be created by a man who can rise above the present and is able to dedicate his art to the whole of mankind without regard to race, religion or culture. To be honest, I am more than a little proud that it was possible to secure this great masterpiece by Sir Anthony Caro for the Museum Würth.

REINHOLD WÜRTH
May 1999

Anthony Caro and Twentieth-Century Sculpture

above **1**. Auguste Rodin 1840–1917
The Gates of Hell 1880–1917
Zurich, Kunsthaus

opposite **2**. Anthony Caro
The Last Judgement 1995–9
stoneware, jarrah wood and steel
Overall size 384 × 3200 × 740 cm
Installation at the Antichi Granai,
Venice Biennale, 1999
Museum Würth, Künzelsau

'WHAT IF THIS PRESENT were the world's last night?' was the dramatic question posed by John Donne, the distinguished seventeenth-century preacher, poet and philosopher,[1] in one of his *Holy Sonnets*, and Anthony Caro gives his terrifying interpretation of Judgement Day to conclude the remarkable history of twentieth-century sculpture that opened with Rodin's *Gates of Hell* [**1**].[2]

Caro's *Last Judgement* [**2**] is the latest episode in a series of multi-part sculptures which the artist has created in recent years. The series began in the late eighties with *After Olympia*, 1986–7 [**21**] a sculpture normally sited in Paris but exhibited in Rome in 1992 as part of an exciting – and memorable – exhibition of Caro's work that was set in the great hall of the Trajan Markets.[3] The parts that make up this steel sculpture are assembled on one base, just as they are in the classical pediment of Olympia to which the artist is making reference.

In 1993 and 1994 *The Trojan War* [**7**] followed.[4] This work consists of forty separate sculptures. It includes the gods of Olympus, the Achaian and Trojan warriors, the *Skaian Gate* and *The Trojan Horse*, the famous trick of Ulysses for taking the city.

The bronze and steel sculptures that Caro created concurrently in the late eighties and early nineties became increasingly more remarkable as they became more architectural: *The Tower of Discovery* 1991 [**4**], *Night Movements* 1987–90, *Cathedral* 1988–9, *First Light* 1990–3 [**5**] etc. The idea of creating works of several separate elements can be regarded as a natural consequence of this endeavor, intensifying the relationship between sculpture and space. This was superbly demonstrated with his

above **3**. Anthony Caro
Promenade 1996
painted steel, overall size 490 × 340 × 450 cm
Installation at the Tuileries Gardens, Paris 1996
Annely Juda Fine Art, London

opposite **4**. Anthony Caro
Tower of Discovery 1991
steel painted, 671 × 554 × 554 cm
Museum of Contemporary Art, Tokyo

right **5**. Anthony Caro
First Light 1990–93
steel, hot zinc sprayed and painted
104 × 223.5 × 195.5 cm
*Solomon R. Guggenheim Foundation,
New York*

sculpture *Promenade* 1996 [**3**], a composition of five individual parts exhibited in Paris in the autumn of 1996 as part of the 'Un Siècle de Sculpture Anglaise' exhibition at the Jeu de Paume.[5]

In 1994, sculptural quality and architectural space were brought together when Caro exhibited in the two large rooms of the Henry Moore Studio in Dean Clough, Halifax.[6] *Halifax Steps 'Spirals'* 1994 [**6**], in steel, reflected the former concept, the latter was evident in two Ziggurats made from railway sleepers. Each work established a dialogue with its respective environment. As a result of this invitation by the Henry Moore Sculpture Trust, Caro was able to fulfill an old aspiration: 'to

7. Anthony Caro
The Trojan War 1993–94
Installation at the Yorkshire Sculpture Park
1994–95

make something of a large size without any need to justify it to committees or to make the compromises which large-scale public sculptures often entail', he told an interviewer at the time.

Before coming to the subject of Anthony Caro's place in contemporary – and not just British – sculpture it may be useful briefly to analyse his most recent work, *The Last Judgement*. This sculpture on the one hand is a summation of fifty years work, on the other hand it lunges deeply into the horror of our troubled times.

One can also see that Caro's approach at the end of the second millennium to the subject of the Last Judgement seems to display the same sort of hellish sadism that Giotto depicted seven hundred years ago in some details of his *Last Judgement* at the Scrovegni Chapel in Padua [8].[8] It is towards this rather than centring Michelangelo's majestic interpretation of the *Last Judgement* on the end wall of the Sistine Chapel that Caro seems to be responding.

Caro's concepts are rooted in literature, ranging from the ancient Homer, Virgil and Dante to philosophers and English poets such as John Donne, Robert Burton, Thomas Browne, James Joyce and T. S. Eliot.[9] For example this reference from *Paradise Lost* by John Milton seems appropriate:

> *The mind is its own place, and in it self*
> *Can make a Heav'n of Hell, a Hell of Heav'n.*

8. Giotto di Bondone *c.*1266–1337
*The Last Judgement c.*1305 (detail)
Scrovegni (Arena) Chapel, Padua

Twenty-five sculptures constitute the apocalyptic new Valley of Jehoshaphat in Caro's *Last Judgement*. A search for precedents for multi-part sculptures presented as one work would probably lead us to the Elgin Marbles, the pediments of Olympia and Aegina, the façades of Romanesque and Gothic cathedrals, Bernini's angels in Castel Sant' Angelo, Canova's funerary monuments and the nineteenth-century French *Commandes Publiques*.[10] An example of similar work by a present-day British sculptor is Barbara Hepworth's *Family of Man*, 1970. This is made up of nine separate bronzes and can be seen today, magical and solitary, amongst the trees on a hillside at the Yorkshire Sculpture Park in West Bretton.

Anthony Caro's revival of the custom of grouping many sculptures together in one narrative cycle is not an isolated practice today. Many young British sculptors who comprise the movement of which Caro is now universally regarded as the founder, have done so as well. They also are spurred on by the ambition to create installation sculptures of many parts.

Caro uses a kind of precise and dramatic narrative context represented by forms that are partly abstract and partly

9. Pablo Picasso 1881–1973
Guernica 1937
Madrid, Museo Nacional Reina Sofia

metaphors of reality. As Caro himself reminded me during a recent conversation we had in London about his *Last Judgement*: 'It is not possible to produce art today with this focus without some sort of visual memory of a supreme work like Picasso's *Guernica* [**9**]. As if by magic, the dichotomy that Caro has used in his sculpture since he was a young man is once again reconstructed in his *Last Judgement*. As I will go on to explore further at a later point, the abstract is able to co-exist peacefully with references to the figure.

The artist obviously takes the entire story of modernity into consideration. He has a sharp and tenacious eye and he is exceptionally knowledgeable about art. His method of breaking down into components – helped by the technique of assemblage – shows that he not only bears *Guernica* very much in mind but that he has worked in the tradition of the Cubist sculptors like Archipenko, Picasso, Lipchitz, Duchamp-Villon and, above all, from the Constructivists like the Russian Tatlin, Gabo, Pevsner, Rodchenko, as well as from a range of Western sculptors including Gonzàlez, David Smith and Calder.[11]

For example, he uses the double bolts of railway sleepers to portray *Charon's* [**12**] passengers 'Those tired and naked souls'.[12] These 'ready-made' materials accentuate the feeling of unease created by the empty eye-like sockets. He is reminiscent of Goya when he presents a hanged man before a pitiless crowd [**13**]. The horns in *Hell is a City* are symbols of the deafening noises that disturb the peace in our modern cities and ruin our ability to concentrate. And the brothel scene *Flesh* reminds us of the *'croquis-bête'* given by Emile Bernard to Van Gogh which became the inspiration for his *Café de Nuit à Arles* [**10**], painted in 1888.[13] In fact Caro based the shape of his tables with skulls and animals, on the billiard table in this café painting [**11**].

The entrance is through the *Bell Tower* reminiscent of the contours of the Mycenaean Lion gate. Above the door there is a metaphoric reference to Hemingway's warning about the Spanish Civil War: 'For Whom the Bell Tolls'. We then come to

10. Vincent van Gogh 1853–1890
Café de Nuit à Arles 1888
Collection Yale University Gallery, New Haven

11. Anthony Caro
Still Life – Skulls 1996–99
stoneware, jarrah wood and oak
155 × 111 × 152 cm
Museum Würth, Künzelsau

opposite **12.** Anthony Caro
Charon 1996–99
stoneware, jarrah wood and steel, 208 × 123 × 101.5 cm
Museum Würth, Künzelsau

above **13.** Anthony Caro
Without Mercy 1996–99
stoneware, jarrah wood and steel, 219 × 126 × 86 cm
Museum Würth, Künzelsau

the *Door of Death*, ajar but blocked. Beyond there is unfathomable mystery, weighed down by the burden of tragedy and death.

The work is surprising and thought-provoking. Throughout *The Last Judgement* the detailed succession of abstract and narrative unfolds inevitably. Each event is a sort of box made of iron and wood. The mixture of materials (used by Constructivists and mentioned in the 1920 *Realist Manifesto* by Gabo and Pevsner) is surprisingly barbaric, and there is probably a reference in the boxes to Tatlin's 'Counter Reliefs'. The steel is bluish in colour, the wood (Australian *jarrah*) has a pinkish patina and the stoneware clay of the impenetrable kind is moulded at high temperatures in a wood kiln which adds a black patina to the ochre of the clay.

At the end, in front of the Eden door, trumpets announce the land of the Just [**14**]. Between these and the *Door of Death* are episodes from Homer (*Tiresias*, prophet of misfortune), from Dante (*Charon*, the ferryman of the souls of the damned) and from the Bible (*Jacob's Ladder*, *Salomé Dances*) together with

14. Anthony Caro
The Last Trump and
The Gate of Heaven 1996–9
stoneware, jarrah wood and steel
Installation at the Antichi Granai,
Venice Biennale, 1999
Museum Würth, Künzelsau

references to existentially contemporary events. Caro recognises our mortal tragedies and the failings of humanity, both ancient and modern: war and genocide – the killing fields, violence, greed, betrayal and hypocrisy. The latter episode, a direct reference to Giotto and the fresco of St Francis at Assisi where he is depicted holding up a crumbling church [15].

And incidentally, Giotto was also the source of Caro's inspiration for a recent series of sculptures, the Arena pieces. The first, *Arena Piece Beginning* 1995 [16], created in 1995, is a referral to Giotto's *Pala d'Ognissanti* in the Uffizi. Modern Art is given new direction by the intensity and effect of Giotto's careful balance in space of architecture and figures – decidedly human figures. With its Brancusian leanness, Caro's sculpture symbolises the beginning of life.[14]

above **15.** Giotto di Bondone *c.*1266–1337
The Dream of Innocent III 1296–97
Detail of the St Francis Fresco
San Francesco, Upper Church, Assisi

right **16.** Anthony Caro
Arena Piece Beginning 1995
wood and steel painted, 72 × 54 × 38 cm
Private Collection, USA

opposite **17**. Anthony Caro
Installation view of the first exhibition of
coloured abstract floor based sculpture at
the Whitechapel Gallery, London 1963

above **18**. Alexander Calder 1898–1976
Teodelapio 1962
City of Spoleto

THE MAN WHO CREATED *The Last Judgement* is the artist who, since the sixties, has done far more than just change the direction and significance of British sculpture.

When his first abstract sculptures were exhibited in London in 1963 [**17**],[15] the brightly painted and intersecting geometric steel plates, iron girders and mesh taken from steelyards were regarded as shocking. But young artists were able to see the completely different spatial impact that this new three-dimensional work could make and his sculptures were met with enthusiasm. The academic pedestal was no more. No more the spectator's enforced viewpoint. The eternal dilemma – the relationship between mass and void – had disappeared. Sculpture had been revitalised and had *another* presence, very different from the constructed works by artists of the earlier avant-garde.

Although still fairly unknown at that time, only the great *stabiles* by Alexander Calder (the first, on a huge scale and painted black was *Teodelapio* [**18**], made in 1962 for Spoleto) maintained as much formal freedom. And in the United States, just before his tragic death, David Smith had begun to paint his last sculptures.[16]

The originality and architectural splendour that distinguish Anthony Caro's first abstract works are undoubtedly American in origin, and he has always received considerable critical acclaim.[17] Soon after he won the sculpture prize at the Paris Biennale for young artists in 1959, two decisive events occurred in Caro's life to change the course of his art. The first was his London meeting with the American critic Clement Greenberg, one of the greatest champions of the new art. The

second was his visit to the United States where he met the sculptor David Smith and the painter Kenneth Noland. Their influence could be detected just one year later with Caro's first abstract sculpture, *Twenty-Four Hours* [20].

Caro had begun to paint his sculptures and his choice of colour was surprising. He used various brands of paint, often adopting their names as titles for his works (*Pompadour*, as in the colour chart title Pompadour Pink). He created completely new and original combinations, for example green with blue and brown for *Sculpture Seven* 1961, the vivid red of *Early One Morning* 1962 [19], the chrome yellow of *Midday* 1960, the magenta, orange and green of *Month of May* 1963 and the mustard yellow of *Sun Feast* 1969–70.[18] No other display of multi-coloured works will ever compare with his extraordinary exhibition in Rome in 1992, on the terraces of the Trajan Markets, overlooking the Forum and Palatine Hill [22].

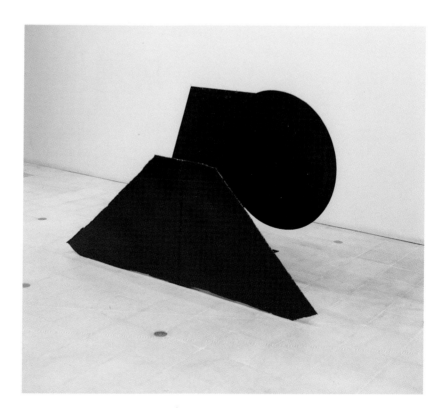

opposite **19.** Anthony Caro
Early One Morning 1962
steel and aluminium painted, 290 × 620 × 33 cm
The Tate Gallery, London

right **20.** Anthony Caro
Twenty-Four Hours 1960
steel painted, 138.5 × 223.5 × 89 cm
The Tate Gallery, London

opposite **21**. Anthony Caro
After Olympia 1986–87
steel rusted and varnished
332.5 × 2342 × 170 cm
Installation at the Trajan Markets, Rome 1992
EPAD, *La Defense, Paris*

above **22.** Anthony Caro
The Trajan Markets, Rome
Retrospective exhibition 1992

DURING THE EARLY FIFTIES Caro had worked as Henry Moore's assistant at Much Hadham. During these periods of close contact with the great sculptor, he learned to pay particular attention to the treatment of materials. At the time Caro was modelling and casting figurative sculptures as well as producing intense drawings, including female nudes, using a variety of media including pastels and ink [24] (just as David Smith had done for the *Bolton Landing Girls* series).[19] However, his training with Moore was more technical and professional than stylistic, and by the time Caro left he was already paying greater attention to the works of Picasso, Dubuffet, De Kooning and the distorted figures of art nègre.

His acquaintance with America therefore came just at the right time, and he became involved with David Smith and his circle of artists: Noland, Olitski and Frankenthaler, as well as Stella and Poons who gravitated towards Bennington, Vermont, where Caro had obtained a three-year teaching post in the college and which was also close to Bolton Landing in upstate New York where Smith lived.

Caro's American experience caused his work to undergo a 'breakthrough',[20] and this change sparked what later became known as 'the quiet revolution of British Sculpture'.[21]

With his new works came a rethink, a concept of the renewal of sculpture. Having absorbed David Smith's ideas, Caro went further and he became recognised as the most accomplished European and American sculptor. His abstract works occupied space in a different way from that of Smith or Gonzàlez (or even Picasso). During a period when the abstract reigned supreme, his works (to quote Greenberg) were 'integrally abstract'.

Caro added his own personal syntax, developing his works on a horizontal plane to achieve a harmony despite the boldness of the articulated arrangements. What appeared to be a casual *assemblage* was in fact deeply felt and articulated.

And yet ... the expressive *côté*, which is to say the narrative and descriptive that sustained Caro in his early years, some critics say, never fully disappeared. They feel it has remained evident in his *assemblages* of materials mostly collected from steelworks (some salvaged from David Smith's studio after his death in 1965) and in works made of scrap metal similar in shape to real objects or cut geometric forms such as *Midnight Gap* 1976–8, *Odalisque* 1983–4, and *The Soldier's Tale* 1983 [25] executed in the seventies and eighties.

His desire to create an expression of feeling accounts for the dichotomy of Caro's art, his method of proceeding along two lines, of alternating between the abstract and the real often working in both modes at the same time. Exactly the same can be said of Picasso's sculpture (and painting). When interviewed in 1961 by Lawrence Alloway,[22] Caro spoke of his aversion to expressionist models and said that this type of figure in his work had begun to disappear even before he went to the United States. 'America', he said, 'was the catalyst for a change in my work. There's a fine-art quality about European art even when it's made of junk. America made me see that there are no barriers and no regulations. Americans simply aren't bound to traditional or conventional solutions in their art or anything else ... There is a tremendous freedom in knowing that your only limitation in a sculpture or painting is whether it's art'. But from this we must deduce that his rejection is a reference only to the history of sculpture up to Picasso's *Guitar* in 1912. From then on history belongs to him which is why, as the twentieth century comes to a close, Caro is regarded as the supreme sculptor of the past forty years.

25. Anthony Caro
The Soldier's Tale 1983
steel patinated and painted, 183 × 208 × 134.5 cm
The Tate Gallery, London

WHEN HE RETURNED TO LONDON from the United States, Caro continued teaching part-time at St Martin's School of Art on Charing Cross Road [**26**]. From the early sixties onwards, British art schools in London helped play a decisive role in the radical changes that were taking place in art.[23] The Royal College directed by Bernard Meadows, the Royal Academy Schools and the Slade were also breeding grounds for change. Although the 1968 student demonstrations that erupted in art academies and schools elsewhere in Europe had little following in Britain, there were significant artists among the coterie of teachers and promising students which helped overwhelm resistance and so brought a change from the old traditional academic way of teaching.

At St Martin's teachers and students talked on equal terms. Their main topics for discussion were new sculpture techniques and new materials and new ways of thinking about and seeing sculpture.

The sculpture of Epstein and Gaudier-Brzeska, Hepworth, Ben Nicholson and Henry Moore came under review. Importance was attributed to the relationship between viewer and artwork and the role of sculpture as an urban expression.

Despite resistance on the part of the academics, the 1962 *Sculture nella città* exhibition in Spoleto had a huge knock-on effect in Britain. It was much talked about in newspaper and magazine articles. David Sylvester, somewhat of a pioneer, enthusiastically reviewed the exhibition in an article for the *Sunday Times* entitled 'The Spoleto Experiment', and included large colour photographs. Many of the most important sculptors of the Henry Moore generation exhibited at

28. Phillip King
Brake 1968
British Council Collection

Spoleto together with others of various nationalities. This was where David Smith became known in Europe for his twenty-six *Voltri* sculptures, assembled together in the Roman amphitheatre of this city in Umbria [27]. Calder's *Teodelapio* [18] found a permanent home here.[24]

Phillip King [28] and Tim Scott [29] were with Caro at St Martin's, but both were about ten years younger than their colleague. David Annesley, Michael Bolus, William Tucker, Isaac Witkin, Barry Flanagan, Richard Long, Richard Deacon [31] and Gilbert and George were among the students, and many came back to teach. No ordinary school then, but a veritable foyer of artists that easily took on the mantle of a collective avant-garde *atelier*. Each and every one was free to speak his mind and to work in an open way in that democratic and fast-moving hothouse where intelligent discussions took place as sculptures were created. On Caro's recommendation, a welding shop was set up in 1960.

In 1963, Sir Herbert Read the respected art historian wrote an article in which he expressed the general surprise aroused by the arrival of a new type of British sculpture and considered the repercussions throughout the world. Although at that time he was still of the classical way of thinking and therefore more inclined towards Moore and Hepworth, Read's promising view of the new generation of sculptors added weight to their argument.

However, Sir Herbert's 'new generation' was still the middle generation of Adams, Armitage, Chadwick, Meadows, Butler and Eduardo Paolozzi (only the latter a contemporary of Caro). The concept of *quality* in art was still in force and respected.

The artists all took part in the first open-air exhibition in Battersea Park, reviewed by Read. There were British and Americans, including both Caro and David Smith, but Sir Herbert had muted opinions of them.

Three years later, in 1966, a second open-air exhibition

took place in the same London park and became as famous as Middleheim, near Antwerp, for this type of sculpture installation. The exhibition was introduced by Alan Bowness and it was on this occasion, as Charles Harrison wrote, that 'the focus of attention fell on the works of Caro and of some younger sculptors who had clearly been subject to his influence'.[25] The second exhibition contained works by British sculptors only, with just one work by David Smith as a tribute to the American who had died in the interim. 'If there was one factor that united this latter group of artists, it was their determined opposition to just that form of contained and imposing monumentality which Read had asserted as a necessary condition of *quality* in sculpture, and which was associated, above all, with the work of Moore.'

Caro carried on teaching at St Martin's for a long time, exerting great influence on at least two generations of artists.[26] Meanwhile his own work was gradually changing. He travelled frequently to America and worked often near to Bennington. Although he distanced himself, he came very close to the ideas of American Minimalism. In America Caro

29. Tim Scott
Quinquereme 1966–67
The Tate Gallery, London

learned to successfully develop his intuition, enabling him to create constructivist sculpture and to use industrial materials. Picasso, the Russians, Gonzàlez and Smith had used a Constructivist method, albeit with other formal elements. And together with Caro there was Jacobson in Denmark, Stankiewicz in America, some young Italian sculptors, Franchina, Consagra and the older Colla.

Many of Caro's colleagues of all nationalities benefited from the importance of these new developments, but it was young British artists in particular who were most stimulated – often in thoughtful opposition to Caro's views. Tony Cragg, Richard Deacon, Bill Woodrow, Richard Long and Rachel Whiteread were all witness to a complete break with the past and it was Caro who showed them that the point of departure could be different. This questioning approach (rather than any discreet respect) was their starting point.

Many of these artists then took their own art in a different direction with some keeping to the conceptual, some following Minimalism or Performance Art, some turning to nature and others using irony in support of Body Art (like Gilbert and George). Even a young American like Charles Ray [30], later noted for his dazzling and childlike plastic nudes, began to explore the 'tension, balance and serialisation', formal qualities

30. Charles Ray
Untitled 1971
Courtesy Regen Projects,
Los Angeles

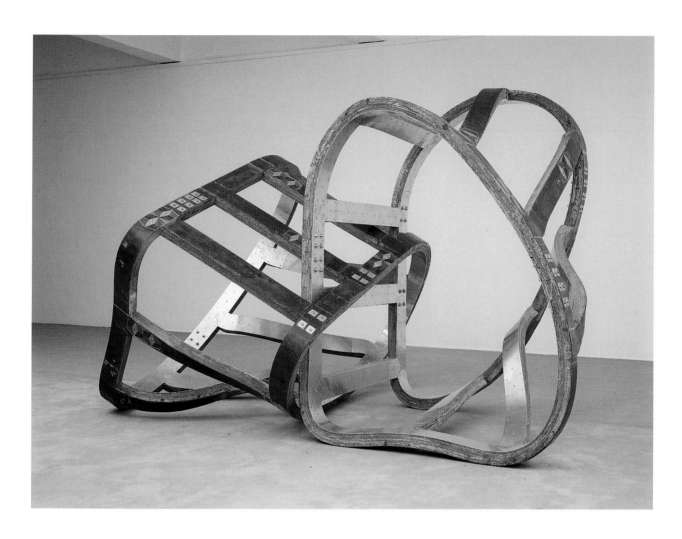

31. Richard Deacon
Lock 1990
Weltkunst Foundation, Zurich

present in Caro's work during the sixties, and the influence could be seen in his Iowa City installation in 1971. Ray was introduced to Caro's work by Roland Brener who had been Caro's student at St Martin's.[27]

In the seventies Caro started to use steel in a way which respected the properties of the material. This started with an excellent opportunity in Italy, in Brianza, where he used roll end steel to create a series of imposing works. He was able to repeat the experience again but with thicker steel near Toronto in Canada and also in England where he had set up a large, well-equipped *atelier*.

32. Anthony Caro
Curtain Road 1974
steel rusted and varnished, 198 × 475.5 × 277 cm
Private Collection, USA

It is interesting to note that the flatter contours resulting from the use of the raw sheet metal he worked with in these places was to become a stylistic factor of his work. Unusual angles and increasingly composite structures began to emerge, with concave and rigid forms alternating between the architectural and the graphic, to enrich the expressive range of his refined yet powerful language.

Using *objets trouvés* procured from the steelworks, huge sheets of steel and odd bits of industrial scrap, he created a new genre of sculpture. When unpainted, the material was crude and rough, given an organic quality by the reddish patina of the rust. From then on steel regained serious importance as a medium due to its prolonged exposure in Caro's repertoire.

Although he used the interwoven and composite metal motif for some time, Caro was always restrained and discerning and hc remained distant from any form of decorative art. His seventies sculptures – *Curtain Road* 1974 [**32**], *Criss Cross Flats* 1974, and *Riviera* 1971–4 are just a few examples – combine the linearity of the cut-out with structural mass. They are both elegant shapes in space and at the same time a solid three-dimensional statement. Like the freshness and grace of a Matisse, the artist's inventiveness seems inexhaustible.

Caro has always admired both Picasso and Matisse. His respect for Matisse's *papiers decoupés* is revealed in early works like *Orangerie* 1969 [**34**]. It was as though he had transcribed a painted work into a three-dimensional object by substituting blowtorch and shears for paintbrush and scissors. More or less the same thing happened during the early thirties when Calder transformed his linear drawings into spatial wire sculptures.

With his *Table Pieces* [**35, 36**], Caro began experimenting with a new way of presenting sculpture. David Smith included three small-scale pieces, *Voltri XVI, XVII* [**33**] and *XIX*,

33. David Smith 1906–65
Voltri XVII 1962

37

above **34.** Anthony Caro
Orangerie 1969
steel painted red, 225 × 162.5 × 231 cm
Private Collection, USA

opposite **35.** Anthony Caro
Table Piece XXII 1967
steel sprayed jewelescent green, 25.4 × 80 × 68.8 cm
Private Collection, UK

in his series of Voltri sculptures: two are placed on four iron legs, the third on an upright plane on four wheels. 'They are nothing', I wrote in 1964, 'but collections of anvils, clamps, spiral springs' that lie inert on the plane.[28] In his book written in 1975 dedicated to Caro's work, William Rubin was the first to draw attention to the connection between these sculptures and Caro's *Table Pieces*, adding also the 1933 Surrealist *Table* by Giacometti. It must be said that Caro made full use of the new and original idea that David Smith so surprisingly added to the story of abstract sculpture. With so much talent and variety, he turned it into his own invention. Over a period of thirty years, the *Table Pieces* have sprung from an endless supply of creativity and appeared in a wide variety of forms: spatial designs precariously balanced on a plane; *assemblages* or source sculptures reminiscent of works by other artists, *after* Mantegna, Leonardo, Picasso and Matisse.

Throughout the long period of time during which Caro developed his work many other innovations became apparent. As he increasingly explored different ways of creating new three-dimensional works, each phase gradually disclosed some unexpected aspect to finally produce, in very coherent language, ever diverse and ever surprising sculpture. Caro always kept well away from simple gestural rhetoric in the various periods of his art.

Meanwhile Caro's work extended to further investigations of form. During the eighties, his controlled improvisation of heavy and amorphous material changed as he became challenged by the increasingly imposing and solid mass and volume. His work was now paralleled by the poetics of Eduardo Chillida, with his forged iron, and Richard Serra who used similar inventive techniques, and he began to create much larger and more monumental structures.

In 1982 Caro initiated a two week annual workshop for painters and sculptors called 'Triangle' as it was originally open to three nationalities – British, American and Canadian,

36. Anthony Caro
Table Piece 'Banquet' 1995
steel and wood, 164 × 79 × 109 cm
Museum Würth, Künzelsau

37. Anthony Caro
Architectural Village 1987 (destroyed)
in collaboration with Frank Gehry, Sheila Girling,
Jon Isherwood, Paul Lubowicki and Susan Nardulli

and took place in Pine Plains, New York State. His interest in creating structures to dominate space naturally led the sculptor to join forces with some of the finest architects. In 1987 the 'Triangle workshop', as it became called, included architects and Caro and Frank Gehry, now noted for his imaginative and futuristic buildings, worked on a sculptural village together (that was subsequently destroyed) [**37**].

Like Gehry, Richard Rogers had great fellowship with Caro even since the St Martin's days. In his introduction to the first of many exhibitions of Caro's sculptures at the Annely Juda Gallery in London, Rogers wrote that both architects and sculptors hold dialogue with mass and implication, adding that Caro 'had literally forged a new language out of simple materials'.[29] Caro has also collaborated with other architects including Tadao Ando and most recently with Sir Norman Foster on the new Millennium bridge that will span the Thames from the New Tate Gallery of Modern Art to St Paul's Cathedral.

Caro said that regardless of the hardness of the material, the process of leaving the external surfaces rough while polishing and hollowing out the internal is the same process used in architecture. From this point of view, recent works by both Caro and Chillida are very much in keeping with each other. With *Monumento a los Fueros* in Vitoria, Chillida takes the same problems of the relationship between external and internal, between sculpture and architecture that Anthony Caro has also treated. Both regard the inside and outside of a sculpture to be inseparable components of one concept. In the *Tower of Discovery* 1991 [4], an environmental sculpture (that you can climb to the top of),[30] Caro has incorporated all parameters necessary for sculpture in one global operation: form and space, volume and mass, gravity and weight and the physical involvement of the spectator. He has added an additional, moral dimension with his latest work, *The Last Judgement*, and from it has emerged a grave indictment of our present day.

'It takes a great artist to start a tradition', said William Rubin in his text on Caro.[31] Almost throughout recent history, constructed rather than moulded sculpture has experienced some moments of insecurity. Picasso was the first with his *Guitar* in 1912, followed by the Russian Constructivists (it may be that Tatlin saw this work when he visited Picasso's studio during his trip to Paris in 1913). Materials and forms totally removed from the basic premises of sculpture that had been in use since ancient times were now in play. New aesthetics had been born. Gonzàlez endorsed Picasso's work when he revealed the plasticity of iron to twentieth-century art. This new concept then fell into disuse until reinvented by Calder and David Smith.

Anthony Caro was the first to demonstrate a clear new direction. It is important to note that he did this at a crucial moment in his career as an artist, in a nation that had scoffed at Epstein and where the growing fame of Henry Moore and his form of Classicism then dominated.

Without Caro's works, British sculpture during the latter half of the twentieth century would have been drowned by academicism. Around the same time as Picasso (1913), Duchamp was also experiencing the same troubles as the Constructivists with his ready-made materials. Not just because of the reaction to Synthetic Cubism and Post-Futurism, but because he was using industrial material and everyday objects. Today Dadaism, a movement which has had a great following from artists all over the world, is very fashionable. However sculpture seen as an object of beauty, with forms that have a challenging presence in space, remains one of the most important aspects that art has known for thousands of years.

Fortunately, Caro's sculpture has guaranteed its continued survival.

Notes and References

1. John Donne (London circa 1573–1631) gradually converted from Catholicism, the religion in which he had been educated, to the Anglican faith. In 1601 he wrote the metaphysical poem *Of the Progress of the Soul* and in 1608 his prose work *Biathanatos*, on the legitimacy of suicide. The *Holy Sonnets*, written in 1618, and his famous sermons delivered in St Paul's Cathedral where he was Deacon, published posthumously, made him famous among his contemporaries. It was T. S. Eliot who drew him from the obscurity into which he had fallen for three centuries.

2. In 1880, the French Minister of Fine Arts commissioned Rodin to make a sculpture for the doorway of the entrance to the new Museum of Decorative Arts. This became *The Gates of Hell*, a monumental but unfinished work exuding immense energy. Details within the work, like *The Thinker*, *The Three Shadows* and *The Kiss* later became independent sculptural figures.

3. Cf. Giovanni Carandente, *Anthony Caro*, published by Fabbri, Milan 1992, Id. *Caro at the Trajan Market*, ed. Ian Barker, Lund Humphries, London 1993. *After Olympia* is an abstract reinterpretation of the west pediment of the Temple of Zeus at Olympia, housed in the Olympia Museum.

4. Cf. *The Trojan War. Sculptures by Anthony Caro*. Texts by John Spurling and Julius Briant, Lund Humphries, London 1994.

5. *Un Siècle de Sculpture Anglaise*, exhibition catalogue, Galerie Nationale du Jeu de Paume, Paris, 1996. Texts by Daniel Abadie and others among which see: Marcelin Pleynet, 'Caro et King dans les Années 60' and Bryan Robertson, 'Caro et la Transformation de la Sculpture dans les Années 60'.

6. The Henry Moore Studio was never a studio of Moore's but became the name of the space (part of the Dean Clough Mill, Halifax) where artists have been invited by the Henry Moore Sculpture Trust to create a special work in response to the space. It has recently been renamed the Henry Moore Foundation Studio.

7. Cf. *Anthony Caro Halifax Steps*, with an interview by Robert Hopper, Director of the Henry Moore Sculpture Trust, Leeds, The Henry Moore Institute, 1995.

8. Giotto's fresco of the Last Judgement on the bottom right-hand-side contains crudely realistic scenes to describe the punishment inflicted on the damned. The naked eye can barely make out the minute and distant details, but the sadistic cruelty portrayed by the artist is none-the-less perturbing, although it has never been emphasised.

9. Robert Burton (1577–1640), clergyman of Oxford, author of *The Anatomy of Melancholy*, a complex work containing many Greek and Latin quotes and tinged with humour. Milton, Sterne, the moralist Laurence Johnson and Charles Lamb all used the work

for their own writing. Thomas Browne (1605–1682), author of *Religio Medici*, one of the first treatise on the relationship between science and religion. For James Joyce, see the stream of consciousness Dedalus from *A Portrait of the Artist as a Young Man*, published in New York in 1916, in which the writer refers to hell as a prison much worse than those on earth.

10. Cf. *La Sculpture Française au XIXe Siècle*, Galerie Nationale du Grand Palais, Paris 1986. Cf. Anne Pingeot, 'Les Commandes Publiques Politiques', pages 162–193 and Catherine Chevillot, 'Les Commandes Publiques Réligieuses', pages 196–251.

11. Cf. *Picasso and the Age of Iron*, edited by Carmen Giménez, with texts by Dore Ashton and Francisco Calvo Serraler, Guggenheim Museum, New York 1993.

12. Dante, *Inferno*, Canto III

13. *Café de Nuit à Arles*, Yale University Gallery, New Haven (another version in a private collection) was Van Gogh's answer to his friend Emil Bernard who, in June 1888, gave him a drawing of a brothel scene. Van Gogh originally intended to reciprocate by making his own painting of the same subject. However, he soon discovered it would be too expensive to paint it from life so he painted the *Café de Nuit à Arles.*

14. The sculpture, in wood and painted steel, is the first of a series of twenty, all of which are quite

small in size. Caro contemplates the creativity in Giotto's work, then uses abstract elements to reinterpret his amazing sense of perspective and the realism of his figures. John Golding, *Caro at the National Gallery – Sculpture from Painting*, London 1998, analyses the sculptor's interest in painting of all periods ranging from the great masters – Mantegna, Leonardo, Rubens, Rembrandt, Manet, Van Gogh, Matisse, Picasso – to contemporary artists like Noland, Morris Louis, Clifford Still, and Frankenthaler.

15. His first one-man exhibition of fifteen abstract sculptures took place in 1963 in the Whitechapel Art Gallery, London, directed at the time by Bryan Robertson, with catalogue text by Michael Fried.

16. Some of David Smith's sculptures were painted after his death. The white coat of primer paint was removed after a decision by the Smith Trustees because it was not the intended final colour. This caused much controversy.

17. In the fifties David Sylvester, Lawrence Alloway, Seuphor and Trier, in the sixties Michael Fried, John Russell, Alan Solomon, Greenberg, Kramer, Bryan Robertson, Rosalind Krauss, in the seventies Spurling, Carmean, Elderfield, Karen Wilkin and William Rubin, and more recently Diane Waldman, Dominique Fourcade, Terry Fenton, and others quoted in these notes and text together with the greatest experts in contemporary art have all highlighted the important position

held by Caro's new sculpture in the latter half of the twentieth century. There is a catalogue raisonné of the entire *opus* compiled by Dieter Blume. Twelve volumes have been published to date.

18. As the artist himself said, it was often his wife, the fine painter Sheila Girling, who advised on colours.

19. In 1996 the Angers Museum mounted a large exhibition of his figurative sculptures and drawings. Catalogue text by Patrick Le Nouëne and Jane Lee.

20. Cf. Clement Greenberg, *Anthony Caro in Art yearbook 8: Contemporary Sculpture*, New York 1965, pages 106–109.

21. Cf. *Quiet Revolution. British Sculpture since 1965*. Catalogue with text by various authors. New York-London, Thames & Hudson, 1987.

22. Lawrence Alloway, Interview with Anthony Caro in *Gazette*, London no.1, 1961, p.1.

23. Cf. Veronique Béranger, 'L'enseignement de la sculpture dans les Écoles d'art Anglaises', in *Un siècle de sculpture Anglaise*, pages 413–20.

24. 'The Sculture nella citta' exhibition, organised by Giovanni Carandente for the V Festival dei Due Mondi, Spoleto 1962, comprised 106 sculptures by 53 artists. There were no means to produce a catalogue, but thirty years later a book was written by Giovanni

Carandente and illustrated with wonderful photographs by Ugo Mulas: Cf. Giovanni Carandate, *Una citta piena di sculture. Spoleto 62*, Electa Editori Umbri, Perugia 1992.

25. Cf. Charles Harrison, 'Sculpture's Recent Past' in *Quiet Revolution*, pp.10–33.

26. The influence that Caro's new sculpture exerted is evident in so many artists' work, including his students Barry Flanagan, David Annesley, Michael Bolus, Issac Witkin, Bill Woodrow, Katherine Gili, David Evison, Peter Hyde and Jeff Lowe, and his colleagues at St Martin's like King and Scott whose early works – *Call* 1967 and *Brake* 1968 [**28**] by King, and *Quinquereme* 1966–7 [**29**] and *Bird in Arras* 1968 by Scott – are very similar in many ways to works by Caro at that time. Richard Deacon, who at 50 is one of the best-known sculptors in Britain today, was also motivated by Caro's sculpture at that time as can be seen in his early works like *Untitled* 1975 (*Quiet Revolution*, p.75), consisting of sheets of formica, plaster and laminated plastic, and *Lock* 1990 [**31**]. Cf. *British Sculpture in the Twentieth Century*, ed. by Sandy Nairne and Nicholas Serota, Whitechapel Art Gallery 1981; *The Sculpture Show. Fifty Sculptors at the Serpentine Gallery and the South Bank*, mounted by Paul de Monchaux, Fenella Chricton and Kate Blacker, London 1983; and for the younger generation, and in addition to publications already mentioned – *Quiet Revolution* and *Un Siècle de Sculpture Anglaise* – please see the catalogue of the exhibition *British Art of the 1980s and the 1990s – Breaking the Mould*, The Weltkunst Collection, mounted by Catherine Marshall with text by Richard Cork and Penelope Curtis, Lund Humphries, London 1997.

27. Cf. Paul Schimmel, *Charles Ray*, The Museum of Contemporary Art, Los Angeles 1998. Text by Schimmel and Lias Phillips. A piece created in 1978 by Ray may be of interest as this was the period when his work was half way between Minimalism and Performance Art. The work is entitled *In Memory of Moro*, dedicated to the Italian statesman who was kidnapped and killed by the Red Brigade. An arm holding a red flag emerges from an empty cube, painted red (was Ray familiar with the work of Francesco Lo Savio?). Ray's work has often been reviewed in Giancarlo Politi's magazine *Flash Art* which dedicated its cover to the artist in 1992.

28. Cf. Giovanni Carandente, *David Smith. Voltron*, photos by Ugo Mulas and David Smith, Institute of Contemporary Art of Pennsylvania, Abrams, New York 1964. The Italian version of this text is published in the exhibition catalogue for the David Smith exhibition at the Fondazione Prada, Charta, Milan 1995.

29. Cf. *Aspects of Anthony Caro. Recent Sculpture 1981–89*, Introduction by Richard Rogers, Annely Juda Fine Art & Knoedler Gallery, London 1989. On the relationship between Caro's work and architecture, see Paul Moorhouse, *Sculpture towards Architecture*, Tate Gallery, London 1991.

30. *Tower of Discovery* was preceded in 1984 by a smaller version, *Child's Tower Room*, made of oak, open to children for climbing.

31. William Rubin, *Anthony Caro*, The Museum of Modern Art, New York 1975.

A Biographical Survey

COMPILED BY IAN BARKER

1924   Born 8 March, New Malden, Surrey, England

1937–42   Attends Charterhouse School, Godalming, Surrey

During vacations works in studio of sculptor Charles Wheeler

1942–4   Attends Christ's College, Cambridge; M.A. in Engineering

Attends Farnham School of Art during vacations

1944–6   Fleet Air Arm of Royal Navy

1946–7   Regent Street Polytechnic, London; studies sculpture with Geoffrey Deeley

1947–52   Royal Academy Schools, London, where he receives a strict academic training

Studies and copies Greek, Etruscan, Romanesque and Gothic sculpture

1948   Awarded two silver medals and one bronze medal from Royal Academy Schools for clay figure models, carving and composition

Travels to France in summer, spending a month drawing, photographing and studying Chartres Cathedral

1949   Marries the painter Sheila Girling (two sons Timothy, 1951, and Paul, 1958)

1951–3   Works as part-time assistant to Henry Moore

Anthony Caro with Henry Moore c.1952

1953–79   Teaches two days weekly at St Martin's School of Art, London

Joins Frank Martin, Head of Sculpture Department, in organising the department and developing the curriculum. Integrates sculpture and drawings into a single class with a view to understanding rather than copying the subject

1954   Moves to Hampstead

Models figurative sculpture in clay and plaster that were mainly cast in bronze, including *Man Holding His Foot*

The Hampstead studio c.1955

During summer vacations at Porlock, Somerset, makes moulds of rocks and cliff outcroppings that he incorporates along with pebbles into figurative sculptures

1955   Included in group exhibition of sculpture at 'New Painters and Painter-Sculptors', Institute of Contemporary Arts, London

1956   First one-man exhibition at Galleria del Naviglio, Milan

Twenty sculptures are shown, including *Woman Waking Up* (1955)

1957   First one-man exhibition in London: Gimpel Fils Gallery

1958   *Man Taking off His Shirt* (1955–56) exhibited at the Venice Biennale

1959   Wins sculpture prize at Paris Biennale, sculptures exhibited include *Woman With Flowers* (1958) and *Woman On Her Back* (1951)

Tate Gallery purchases *Woman Waking Up* (1955)

Meets Clement Greenberg in London

Visits USA for the first time on Ford Foundation English Speaking Union Grant; meets Kenneth Noland and David Smith, also Robert Motherwell, Helen Frankenthaler and others

1960   Returns to London

Makes first abstract sculptures in steel including *Twenty-Four Hours* (1960)

Radical change in his ideas forces him to rethink his teaching methods. A welding shop is set up at St Martin's. Experimental atmosphere in school and working relationship with students provide a forum for stimulating exchanges

Visits Carnac, Brittany, studies the menhirs and dolmens

1961   First exhibits a steel sculpture *The Horse* (1961) in 'New London Situtation', Marlborough New London Gallery, London

Makes first polychrome sculpture *Sculpture Seven* (1961)

First one-man exhibition in London at the Gimpel Fils Gallery 1957

With *Sculpture Three* 1961

Anthony Caro standing beneath his sculpture *Sculpture Three* 1962 at the Whitechapel Gallery, London 1963

1963   One-man exhibition of fifteen abstract steel sculptures at Whitechapel Art Gallery, London, organised by director, Bryan Robertson. Sculptures exhibited include *Twenty-Four Hours* (1960), *Midday* (1960), *Sculpture Seven* (1961), *Sculpture Three* (1962), *Early One Morning* (1962), *Month of May* (1963), and *Pompadour* (1963)

1963–5 Teaches at Bennington College, Bennington, Vermont

Renews contact with Noland, Olitski, and Smith. Large garage belonging to Bennington Fire Department is made available for Caro's use as a temporary studio

From left to right: Clement and Jenny Greenberg, Sheila and Anthony Caro, and Kenneth Noland, Bennington 1963

1964   First one-man exhibition in New York at André Emmerich Gallery. Five sculptures shown include *Prospect* (1964)

Exhibits *Month of May* (1963) and *Hopscotch* (1962) at Documenta III, Kassel, Germany

Charlie Hendy becomes Caro's studio assistant

First one-man exhibition in New York at the André Emmerich Gallery 1964

1965   Exhibits *Early One Morning* (1962) in 'British Sculpture in the Sixties', Tate Gallery, London. The Contemporary Art Society presents *Early One Morning* (1962) to the collection of the Tate Gallery

Exhibition at Washington Gallery of Modern Art, Washington DC, includes *Twenty-Four Hours* (1960), *Sculpture Seven* (1961) and *Prospect* (1964)

After 1965 Caro visits USA approximately three times a year, usually returning to work for about a month

1966   Exhibits in 'Five Young British Artists', British Pavilion, Venice Biennale (with painters Richard Smith, Harold Cohen, Bernard Cohen and Robyn Denny)

1966 Exhibits in 'Primary Structures: Younger American and British Sculptors' at the Jewish Museum, New York, organised by Kynaston McShine

Begins first table sculptures following a conversation with Michael Fried

Incorporates grilles and mesh screens into sculptures including *The Window* (1966–7) and *Red Splash* (1966)

1967 Retrospective exhibition at Rijksmuseum Kröller-Müller, Otterlo

Acquires stock of raw materials from estate of David Smith

Exhibits *Prairie* (1967) and *Deep Body Blue* (1967) at Kasmin Ltd, London

1968 Incorporates steel table surfaces into large-scale sculptures including *Trefoil* (1968). Exhibits *Titan* (1964) in 'Noland, Louis and Caro', Metropolitan Museum of Art, New York

Awarded Honorary Doctor of Letters Degree, University of East Anglia

Guest artist at the Thirtieth Annual Exhibition, Contemporary Art Society of New South Wales, Australia

1969 Retrospective exhibition at Hayward Gallery, London. Exhibition consists of fifty works made between 1954 and 1968

Appointed Commander of the Order of the British Empire

Exhibits, with John Hoyland, in British Section of Tenth São Paulo Biennale

Moves studio to former piano factory in Camden Town, London

Purchases parts of agricultural machinery, including plough shares and propeller blades which were used in sculptures incorporating different levels, including *Orangerie* (1969) and *Sun Feast* (1969–70)

Patrick Cunningham becomes Caro's studio assistant

1970 Begins making unpainted steel sculptures, including *The Bull* (1970), assisted by James Wolfe and later Willard Beopple at Shaftsbury, Vermont, in the studio of Kenneth Noland

Exhibits *Pink Stack* (1969) in the exhibition 'Contemporary British Art' at the National Museum of Modern Art, Tokyo

Working at the Ripamonte Steel Factory, Veduggio, Italy 1972

Working at the York Street Factory, Toronto, Canada 1974

1971   Invited to judge Perth prize at Drawing International at Western Australia Art Gallery, Perth, and travels to Mexico, New Zealand, India en route to Australia, lecturing at art schools and universities

1972   Makes a series of seven rusted steel sculptures, the Straight Series, by permutating and developing the structure of one sculpture, *Straight On* (1972)

Makes fourteen sculptures using 'soft edge' Roll End steel at Ripamonte factory, Veduggio, Brianza with James Wolfe as assistant

1973   Obtains soft edge rolled steel from Consett, County Durham, England

One-man exhibition at Norfolk and Norwich Triennial Festival, East Anglia

Museum of Modern Art, New York, acquires *Midday* (1960)

1974   Works at York Steel Co., Toronto, and makes large sculptures using heavy steel handling equipment, such as a gantry and mobile cranes. Completes thirty-seven sculptures which are later known as the Flats Series including *Lake Ontario Flats* (1974), *Pin Up Flat* (1974), *Scorched Flats* (1974) and *Surprise Flats* (1974) assisted by sculptors James Wolfe, Willard Beopple and André Fauteux

Working at the Emma Lake Summer Workshop, University of Saskatchewan, Canada 1977

1975   Retrospective exhibition at Museum of Modern Art, New York (which later travels to Walker Art Center, Minneapolis; Museum of Fine Art, Boston)

Works in ceramic clay at workshop at Syracuse University, New York, organised by Margie Hughto

Begins making sculptures in cast and welded bronze

1976   Presented with key of New York City by Mayor Abraham Beame

1977   Exhibition of table sculptures travels to Tel Aviv Museum, Israel, and later tours to Australia, New Zealand and Germany

Artist in residence at Emma Lake summer workshop, University of Saskatchewan. Sculptures made there are later known as the 'Emma Series', and include *Emma Dipper* (1977) and *Emma Push Frame* (1977/78)

1978   Makes first 'writing pieces': calligraphic sculptures in steel

Executes commission for East Wing of the National Gallery in Washington DC

1979   Receives Honorary Doctorates from the University of East Anglia and York University, Toronto

Made Honorary Member of American Academy and Institute of Arts and Letters, New York

Installation view of the retrospective exhibition at the Museum of Modern Art, New York 1975

1980 Makes a series of bronze screens and first sculptures in lead and wood

1981 Makes wall pieces in handmade paper with Ken Tyler in New York

Receives Honorary Doctorate from Brandeis University, Massachusetts

Exhibits at Städtishe Galerie im Städel, Frankfurt

Made Honorary Fellow, Christ's College, Cambridge

Joins Council of Royal College of Art

1982 Appointed Trustee of Tate Gallery, London

With Robert Loder founded the Triangle Workshop for sculptors and painters at Pine Plains, New York and participates annually thereafter until 1991

Joins Council of Slade School of Art

Working with his assistant Patrick Cunningham in his Camden Town studio, London *c.*1983

1984 One-man exhibition at Serpentine Gallery, London, which travels to Whitworth Art Gallery, University of Manchester; Leeds City Art Gallery; Ordrupgaard Samlingen, Copenhagen; Kunstmuseum, Düsseldorf; Joan Miró Foundation, Barcelona

1984 Completes first sculpture with an architectural dimension: *Child's Tower Room* (1983/84) the Arts Council Commission for 'Four Rooms' exhibition at Liberty's, London

1985 Visits Greece for the first time

Exhibits at Nörrkopings Kunstmuseum, Sweden

Guest lecturer at Sculptors' Workshop, Maastricht

Receives Doctor of Letters, Cambridge University

Jon Isherwood becomes Caro's US studio assistant at Ancram, New York

1986 Completes work on *Scamander* (1986) and *Rape of the Sabines* (1985/86), first of sculptures inspired by Greek pediments

Made Honorary Fellow, Royal College of Art

1987 Awarded Knighthood, Queen's Birthday Honours

Completes *After Olympia* (1986/87), his largest sculpture to date

Attends workshops in Berlin and Barcelona

Receives Honorary Degree, Surrey University

1988 Concludes investigation of pediment-inspired works with *Xanadu*

Awarded Honorary Foreign Membership of the American Academy of Arts and Sciences

After Olympia (1986/87) is installed on roof garden of Metropolitan Museum of Art, New York, for duration of summer

Starts the Catalan Series of thirty-three table sculptures made from steel elements brought back to Caro's studio from the Barcelona workshop

1989 Retrospective exhibition at the Walker Hill Art Center, Seoul

Sculpture workshop, Edmonton

Visits Korea and India

Receives Honorary Degree, Yale University

Begins working on the Cascades Series of fourteen table sculptures which are amongst the largest Caro has made

Exhibits the Barcelona and Catalan Series of sculptures at the Sala de Exposiciones del Banco Bilbao Vizcaya, Barcelona

Working in his Camden Town studio, London *c.*1989

1990   Completes work on *Night Movements* (1987/90) a single work in four separate units

Retrospective exhibition at the Musée des Beaux-Arts, Calais

Awarded Honorary Degree, University of Alberta, Edmonton

Visits Japan and starts series of paper sculptures at Nagatani's workshop, Obama

1991   Two important sculptures involving the dialogue with architecture completed: *Sea Music* (1991) for the quayside, Poole, Dorset and *Tower of Discovery* (1991)

Exhibition of recent work at the Tate Gallery, London (Duveen Gallery) includes *Tower of Discovery*, (1991) *After Olympia* (1986/87), *Xanadu* (1986/88) and *Night Movements* (1987–90)

Awarded first Nobutake Shikanai Prize, Hakone Open-Air Museum, Japan

1991   Exhibits the 'Cascades Table Pieces' showing different selections both at Annely Juda Fine Art, London, and André Emmerich Gallery, New York

1992   Awarded Honorary Membership, Accademia delle belle Arti di Brera, Milan

Tower of Discovery shown at the World Expo Fair, Seville

Obama paper works shown at Fuji Television Gallery, Tokyo

Receives Praemium Imperiale Prize for Sculpture, Tokyo

Retrospective exhibition at the Trajan Market, Rome, organised by Giovanni Carandente and the British Council

1993   Awarded Honorary Degree, Doctor of Letters, Winchester School of Art

Visits France and makes a series of ceramic sculptural elements at the workshop of Hans Spinner near Grasse, which are later combined with wood and steel to form the.*The Trojan War* (1993/94) Series

1993–4 The British Council tours a selection of the Cascades Series to museums in Hungary, Romania, Turkey, Cyprus and Greece

1994–5 Several exhibitions organised to celebrate the artist's 70th birthday, including: *The Trojan War* (1993/94) shown at the Iveagh Bequest, Kenwood, London and Yorkshire Sculpture Park, Wakefield; 'Sculpture Through Five Decades' shown at Annely Juda Fine Art, London, Galerie Hans Mayer, Düsseldorf, and in a modified version at Kukje Gallery, Seoul

Separate exhibitions also held at André Emmerich Gallery, New York, Richard Gray Gallery, Chicago, and Constantine Grimaldis Gallery, Baltimore

Exhibition of table sculptures organised by Kettle's Yard Gallery, Cambridge University, tours to Whitworth Art Gallery, University of Manchester, and Graves Art Gallery, Sheffield

The Henry Moore Sculpture Trust commissions a temporary sculpture installation for the Henry Moore Studio at Dean Clough, Halifax: *Halifax Steps – Ziggurats and Spirals* (1994)

1995   Largest retrospective exhibition held at the Museum of Contemporary Art, Tokyo, curated by Yasuyoshi Saito with special architectural settings by Tadao Ando

1996   Receives Diploma Doctor Honoris Causa, University of Charles de Gaulle, Lille and Honorary Degree, Durham University

Goodwood Steps (1996) displayed at the Hat Hill Sculpture Foundation, Goodwood

1996–7   *The Trojan War* (1993/94) sculptures are shown in Greece at Thessaloniki and at the National Gallery, Athens

From left to right: Yoshishige Saito, Anthony Caro, and Tadao Ando at the opening of the Museum of Contemporary Art, Tokyo retrospective exhibition 1995

View of a corner of the Camden Town studio, London c.1997

With the architect Sir Norman Foster and the engineer Chris Wise, wins the competition for a new footbridge spanning the Thames from St Paul's to the new Tate Gallery of Modern Art at Bankside, London. Schedule for completion in 2000, the bridge is known as the 'Millennium Bridge'

1998   Receives Lifetime Achievement in Contemporary Sculpture Award, International Sculpture Center, Washington DC and Honorary Fine Arts Degree, Florida International University

'Caro: Sculpture from Painting' shown at the National Gallery, London, the first occasion a contemporary sculptor has been invited to exhibit there

Work in Public Collections

Aberdeen Art Gallery

Albright Knox Art Gallery, Buffalo, New York

Aldrich Museum of Contemporary Art,
   Ridgefield, Connecticut

Art Gallery of New South Wales, Sydney

Art Gallery of Ontario, Toronto

Baltimore Museum of Art, Baltimore, Maryland

Bayerische Staatsgemaldesammlung, Munich

City of Barcelona

Bennington College, Bennington, Vermont

Boston Museum of Fine Arts, Massachusetts

Musée des Beaux-Arts, Calais

Carnegie Museum of Art, Pittsburg

Christ's College, Cambridge

Smart Museum, University of Chicago

City of St Louis Museum, Missouri

Cleveland Museum of Art, Cleveland, Ohio

Comino Foundation, USA

Dallas Museum of Fine Arts, Texas

Detroit Institute of Arts, Michigan

Duke University Art Gallery, Durham,
   North Carolina

Dayton Art Institute, Ohio

Edmonton Art Gallery, Alberta

Felton Bequest, Melbourne

Fitzwilliam Museum, Cambridge

Folkwang Museum, Essen

Friends of Johannesburg Art Gallery

Fukuoka City Museum of Art, Japan

Glasgow Museum of Modern Art

Hakone Open Air Museum, Japan

Hirshhorn Museum and Sculpture Garden,
   Smithsonian Institution, Washington DC

Ho-am Art Museum, Seoul

Houston Museum of Fine Arts, Texas

Tibor de Nagy Watson Gallery, Houston

Israel Museum, Jerusalem

J. B. Speed Museum, Louisville, Kentucky

Joan Miró Foundation, Barcelona

Johannesburg Art Gallery

Kaiser Wilhelm Museum, Krefeld

Kunsthalle Bielefeld

Kunsthalle Hamburg

Kunsthalle Mannheim

Kunsthaus, Zurich

Kunstmuseum Hanover (Sammlung Sprengel)

Kunstsammlung der Ruhr-Universität, Bochum

Kunstsammlung Nordrhein-Westfalen,
   Düsseldorf

Los Angeles County Museum of Art, California

Metropolitan Museum of Art, New York

Modern Art Museum of Fort Worth, Texas

Museum of Art, Carnegie Institute, Pittsburgh

Museum Ludwig, Cologne

Museum of Modern Art, New York

Museum of Modern Art Toyama, Toyama City

Museum Schloss Morsbroich, Leverkusen

Museum Würth, Künzelsau

National Gallery of Victoria, Melbourne

National Gallery, Washington DC

National Museum of Art, Osaka

National Museum of Contemporary Art, Seoul

Nelson Gallery of Art, Kansas City, Missouri

Museum of Contemporary Art, Tokyo

North Carolina Museum of Art, Raleigh

Parrish Art Museum, Southampton, New York

Peterborough Development Corporation

Philadelphia Museum of Art, Philadelphia,
Pennsylvania

Phillips Collection, Washington DC

Portland Art Museum, Portland, Oregon

Rijksmuseum Kröller-Müller, Otterlo

Rose Art Museum, Brandeis University, Waltham,
Massachusetts

Sarah Lawrence College, Bronxville, New York

Saarlandmuseum, Saarbrücken

Scottish National Gallery of Modern Art,
Edinburgh

Setagaya Art Museum, Tokyo

Sintra Museum of Modern Art, Portugal
(Berardo Collection)

Skulpturenmuseum Albertinum, Dresden

Solomon R. Guggenheim Museum, New York

Sondra & Marvin Smalley Sculpture Garden,
The Univerity of Judaism, Los Angeles

Staatsgalerie Stuttgart

Storm King Art Centre, Mountainville, New York

Syracuse University, New York

Tate Gallery Foundation, London

Tate Gallery, London

Tel Aviv Museum, Israel

The Arts Council of Great Britain

The British Council, London

The Museum of Modern Art, Toyama

The Museum of Modern Art, Shiga

Toledo Museum of Art, Ohio

UCLA Art Council, Los Angeles, California

Ulster Museum, Belfast

University of Alberta, Edmonton

University of California

University of California, Franklin D. Murphy
Sculpture Garden, Los Angeles

University of East Anglia, Norwich

Vancouver Art Gallery, British Columbia

Von der Heydt Museum, Wuppertal

Wakayama Prefectural Museum, Japan

Wakefield Museum and Art Gallery

Wakita Museum of Art, Japan

Walker Art Center, Minneapolis, Minnesota

Walker Hill Art Center, Seoul

Wallraf-Richartz Museum, Cologne

West London College, London

Westfalisches Landesmuseum, Munster

Whitworth Art Gallery, Manchester

Wilhelm Lehmbruck Museum, Duisburg

Wolfgang Gurlitt Museum / Neue Galerie der
Stadt Linz, Austria

Yale University Art Gallery, New Haven,
Connecticut

York University of Fine Art, Toronto

Selected One-Man Exhibitions

1956 Galleria del Naviglio, Milan

1957 Gimpel Fils Gallery, London

1963 Whitechapel Art Gallery, London

1964 André Emmerich Gallery, New York

1965 Washington Gallery of Modern Art, Washington DC

Kasmin Limited, London

1966 David Mirvish Gallery, Toronto

Galerie Bischofsberger, Zurich

André Emmerich Gallery, New York

1967 Rijksmuseum Kröller-Müller, Otterlo

Kasmin Limited, London

1968 André Emmerich Gallery, New York

1969 Hayward Gallery, London

British Section, X Biennale de São Paulo

1970 André Emmerich Gallery, New York

1971 David Mirvish Gallery, Toronto

Kasmin Limited, London

1972 André Emmerich Gallery, New York

Kasmin Limited, London

1973 André Emmerich Gallery, New York

Norfolk and Norwich Triennial Festival, East Anglia

1974 André Emmerich Gallery, New York

Galerie André Emmerich, Zurich

The Iveagh Bequest, Kenwood, London

Kenwood House, London

David Mirvish Gallery, Toronto

Galleria dell'Ariete, Milan

1975 Museum of Modern Art, New York

Walker Art Center, Minneapolis

Museum of Fine Arts, Houston

1976 Museum of Fine Arts, Boston

Watson de Nagy Gallery, Houston

Galerie Wentzel, Hamburg

Richard Gray Gallery, Chicago

Lefevre Gallery, London

1977 Galerie Piltzer-Rheims, Paris

Waddington and Tooth Galleries, London

André Emmerich Gallery, New York

Tel Aviv Museum, Tel Aviv, and the British Council tour to New Zealand, Australia and Germany

1978 André Emmerich Gallery, New York

Harcus Krakow Gallery, Boston

Knoedler Gallery, London

Galerie André Emmerich, Zurich

Ace Gallery, Venice, California

Antwerp Gallery, Antwerp

Galerie Wentzel, Hamburg

Richard Gray Gallery, Chicago

1979 Kunsthalle Mannheim

Kunstverein Frankfurt

Kunstverein Braunschweig

Städtische Galerie im Lenbachhaus, Munich

Kasahara Gallery, Osaka

Ace Gallery, Vancouver

'Writing Pieces', André Emmerich Gallery, New York

1980 'The York Sculptures', Christian Science Center, Boston (presented by the Boston Museum of Fine Arts, Boston)

Acquavella Contemporary Art, New York

1981 Waddington Galleries, London

Harcus Krakow Gallery, Boston

Storm King Art Center, Mountainville, New York

The Iveagh Bequest, Kenwood, London

Städtische Galerie im Städel, Frankfurt

Downstairs Gallery, Edmonton, Alberta

1982 André Emmerich Gallery, New York

Galerie Wentzel, Cologne

Gallery One, Toronto

Moderne Gallerie im Saarland-Museum, Saarbrücken

Knoedler Gallery, London

1983 Waddington Galleries, London

Knoedler Galleries, London

Galerie de France, Paris

'Anthony Caro Recent Bronzes 1976–81', Municipal Museum, Schiedam

1984 'Anthony Caro 1969–84', Serpentine Gallery, London

Knoedler Gallery, London

Galerie Wentzel, Cologne

Martin Gerard Gallery, Edmonton, Alberta

André Emmerich Gallery, New York

Acquavella Gallery, New York

Whitworth Art Gallery, Manchester

Leeds City Art Gallery, Leeds

Ordrupgaard Samlingen, Copenhagen

1985 Kunstmuseum, Düsseldorf

Joan Miro Foundation, Barcelona

Galerie Wentzel, Cologne

Galerie André Emmerich, Zurich

Constantine Grimaldis Gallery, Baltimore

Gallery One, Toronto
Galerie Blanche, Stockholm
Galerie Lang, Malmö
Galerie Artek, Helsinki
Harcus Gallery, Boston
Galleria Stendhal, Milan
Nörrkopings Kunstmuseum, Sweden

1986 Richard Gray Gallery, Chicago
André Emmerich Gallery, New York
Acquavella Gallery, New York
Galeria Joan Prats, Barcelona
Commune di Bogliasco, Genova
Knoedler Gallery, London
Waddington Galleries, London
Iglesia de San Esteban, Murcia

1986–7 La Lonja, Valencia

1987 Soledad Lorenzo Gallery, Madrid
Constantine Grimaldis Gallery, Baltimore
Northern Centre for Contemporary Art, Sunderland

1987–8 'Bronzes and Drawings', Gallery One, Toronto

1988 'Anthony Caro Paper Sculptures', Sylvia Cordish Fine Arts, Baltimore
Galerie Wentzel, Cologne
Elisabeth Franck Gallery, Belgium
Galerie Renée Ziegler, Zurich
André Emmerich Gallery, New York

1989 André Emmerich Gallery, New York
Constantine Grimaldis Gallery, Baltimore
Sala de Exposiciones del Banco Bilbao Vizcaya, Barcelona
Richard Gray Gallery, Chicago
Kathleen Laverty Gallery, Edmonton
Walker Hill Art Center, Seoul
Nabis Gallery, Seoul
Rutgers Barclay, Santa Fe, New Mexico
Galeria Sebastia Jané, Gerona
Knoedler Gallery, London

Annely Juda Fine Art, London
Fluxus Gallery, Porto
Galeria Acquavella, Caracas

1990 Galeria Charpa, Gandia, Valencia
Galerie Lelong, Paris
Gallery One, Toronto
Musée des Beaux-Arts, Calais
Paribas Bank, Huis Österrieth, Antwerp
Kasahara Gallery, Osaka
Fuji Television Gallery, Tokyo
Pousse Gallery, Tokyo
Asuka Gallery, Tokyo

1991 Tate Gallery, London
Annely Juda Fine Art, London
André Emmerich Gallery, New York
Knoedler Gallery, London
Galerie Hans Mayer, Düsseldorf
Galerie Wentzel, Cologne
Nabis Gallery, Seoul

1992 Ancient Trajan Markets, Rome
Veranneman Foundation, Kruishoutem
Galleria Oddi Baglioni, Rome
Studio Marconi, Milan
Fuji Television Gallery, Tokyo

1993 'Anthony Caro: Cascades'. Touring exhibition organised by The British Council. Exhibiting centres: Mucsarnok, Palme-Haz, Budapest, Hungary; Museum of Art, Cluj, Napoca; Museum of Art, Constant, National Galleries, Bucharest, Roumania; Akbank, Aksanat Art Gallery, Istanbul, State Five Arts Gallery, Ankara, State Painting and Sculpture Museum, Izmir, Turkey; Nicosia Municipal Art Centre, Cyprus

1994 Annely Juda Fine Art, London
Galerie Hans Mayer, Düsseldorf
André Emmerich Gallery, New York
Richard Gray Gallery, Chicago
The Iveagh Bequest, Kenwood, London

Kettle's Yard, Cambridge, then touring to: Whitworth Art Gallery, Manchester and Graves Art Gallery, Sheffield

1994 Constantine Grimaldis Gallery, Baltimore
Kukje Gallery, Seoul
Yorkshire Sculpture Park, Wakefield
Henry Moore Studio, Dean Clough, Halifax

1995 Museum of Contemporary Art, Tokyo (Retrospective)
Galerie Josine Bokhoven, Amsterdam
'Anthony Caro Cascade Sculptures' De Beyerd, Breda
Gallery Kasahara, Osaka
Metropole Arts Centre, Folkestone
Graves Art Gallery, Sheffield

1996 Chesil Gallery, Portland, Dorset (with Sheila Girling)
Galerie Lelong, Paris
Musée des Beaux-Arts, Angers, France
University of Surrey Gallery, Guildford (with Sheila Girling)

1997 Dorset County Museum, Dorchester (with Sheila Girling)
Pier Art Centre, Orkney (with Sheila Girling)
French Institute, Thessaloniki
National Gallery, Athens
Middleheim Sculpture Park, Antwerp

1998 'Sculpture from Painting' National Gallery, London
Annely Juda Fine Art, London
Marlborough Gallery, New York
Galerie Josine Bokhoven, Amsterdam
Kukje Gallery, Seoul
Garth Clark Gallery, New York

1999 Perimeter Gallery, Chicago

Selected Group Exhibitions

1955 'New Sculptors and Painter-Sculptors', Institute of Contemporary Arts, London

'Contemporary Painting and Sculpture', City Art Gallery, Leeds

1956 Summer group exhibition, Gimpel Fils Gallery, London

1957 'Some Younger British Sculptors', Manchester University, Art Department

'Contemporary British Sculpture', open-air touring exhibition arranged by the Arts Council of Great Britain

Summer group exhibition, Gimpel Fils Gallery, London

Summer group exhibition, Redfern Gallery, London

'New Trends in British Art', Rome-New York Art Foundation, Rome

1958 'Contemporary British Paintings, Sculptures and Drawings', British Embassy, Brussels

'Sonsbeek '58: International Exhibition of Sculpture in the Open Air', Sonsbeek Park, Arnhem

'Contemporary British Sculpture', Arts Council of Great Britain

'Three Young English Artists', Central Pavilion, XXIX Venice Biennale

'The Religious Theme', Tate Gallery, London (organised by the Contemporary Art Society, London)

Pittsburgh Bicentennial International Exhibition of Contemporary Painting and Sculpture, Carnegie Institute, Pittsburgh

1959 'First Paris Biennale of Young Artists', Musée d'Art Moderne, Paris

'Fifth Biennale International Exhibition of Sculpture', Middelheim Park, Antwerp

'Biennale International Exhibition of Sculpture', Carrara, Italy

1960 'Contemporary British Sculpture', Arts Council of Great Britain

'Sculpture in the Open Air', Battersea Park, London

1961 'Ten Sculptors', Marlborough New London Gallery, London

'Contemporary British Sculpture', Arts Council of Great Britain

'New London Situation: An Exhibition of British Abstract Art', Marlborough New London Gallery, London

International Union of Architects Congress, London

1962 'Young English Sculptors', Alteneo, Madrid

'Sculpture Today', Midland Group Gallery, Nottingham

1963 'Sculpture: Open-Air Exhibition of Contemporary British and American Works', Battersea Park, London

Group exhibition, Kasmin Limited, London

1964 '1954–1964: Painting and Sculpture of a Decade', Tate Gallery, London

Documenta III, Kassel

'Hampstead Artists 1943–64', Kenwood House, London

1965 'Sculpture from the Arts Council Collection', touring exhibition arranged by the Arts Council of Great Britain

'British Sculpture in the Sixties', Tate Gallery, London

Group exhibition, Kasmin Limited, London

'Sculpture from All Directions', World House Galleries, New York

'Seven Sculptors', Institute of Contemporary Art, University of Pennsylvania, Philadelphia

'Kane Memorial Exhibition', Providence Art Club, Providence, Rhode Island

1966 'Contemporary British Sculpture', Arts Council of Great Britain

'Primary Structures: Younger American and British Sculptors', Jewish Museum, New York

'Sculpture in the Open Air', Battersea Park, London

1966 'Sonsbeek '66: International exhibition of Sculpture in the Open Air', Sonsbeek Park, Arnhem

'Five Young British Artists', British Pavilion, XXXIII Venice Biennale

1967 'Sculpture 60–66', touring exhibition of works from the collection of the Arts Council of Great Britain

'Color, Image, Form', Detroit Institute of Arts, Detroit

'American Sculpture of the Sixties', Los Angeles County Museum

'The 118 Show: Paintings/Constructions/Sculptures/Graphics', Kasmin Limited, London

'The 180 Beacon Collection of Contemporary Art', 180 Beacon Street, Boston

'Englische Kunst', Galerie Bischofberger, Zurich

'Selected Works from the Collection of Mr and Mrs H Gates Lloyd', Institute of Contemporary Art, University of Pennsylvania, Philadelphia

'Guggenheim International Exhibition, 1967: Sculpture from Twenty Nations', Solomon R Guggenheim Museum, New York; shown also during 1968 at the Art Gallery of Ontario, Toronto; National Gallery of Canada, Ottawa; and the Museum of Fine Arts, Montreal

'Pittsburgh International Exhibition of Contemporary Painting and Sculpture', Carnegie Institute, Pittsburgh

1968 'New British Painting and Sculpture', University of California at Los Angeles (organised by the Whitechapel Art Gallery, London); shown also at the University of California Art Museum, Berkeley; Portland Art Museum, Vancouver Art Gallery; Henry Gallery, University of Washington, Seattle; Museum of Contemporary Art, Chicago and Contemporary Arts Museum, Houston

'25 Camden Artists', Camden Arts Festival, London

'Hemisfair '68', San Antonio, Texas

'Noland, Louis and Caro', Metropolitan Museum of Art, New York

'New British Sculpture', open-air and gallery exhibition organised by the Arnolfini Gallery, Bristol

'Sculpture in a City', touring exhibition arranged by the Arts Council of Great Britain

'Sculpture 1960–67', touring exhibition of works from the collection of the Arts Council of Great Britain

'Ways of Contemporary Research', Central Pavilion, XXXIV Venice Biennale

30th Annual Exhibition, Contemporary Art Society of New South Wales, Blaxland Gallery, Sydney

1969 'Between Object and Environment: Sculpture in an Extended Format', Institute of Contemporary Art, University of Pennsylvania, Philadelphia

'Artists from the Kasmin Gallery', Arts Council Gallery, Belfast

'Seven Sculptors', Museum of Modern Art, Oxford

'Stella, Noland, Caro', Dayton's Gallery 12, Minneapolis

1970 Group exhibition, City Art Gallery, Leeds

Group exhibition, Kasmin Limited, London

1970 'British Sculpture out of the Sixties', Institute of Contemporary Arts, London

'Contemporary British Art', The National Museum of Modern Art, Tokyo

'The Opening', David Mirvish Gallery, Toronto

'British Painting and Sculpture 1960–70', National Gallery of Art, Washington DC (organised by the Tate Gallery and The British Council)

1971 Group exhibition, Kasmin Limited, London

'The Deluxe Show', Deluxe Theatre, Houston (sponsored by De Menil Foundation)

Group exhibition, David Mirvish Gallery, Toronto

1972 Group exhibition, David Mirvish Gallery, Toronto

'Contemporary Sculpture: A Loan Exhibition', Phillips Collection, Washington DC

'Six Contemporary English Sculptors', Museum of Fine Arts, Boston

1972 Group exhibition, Kasmin Limited, London

'Masters of the Sixties', Edmonton Art Gallery, Edmonton, Alberta; shown also at Winnipeg Art Gallery; David Mirvish Gallery, Toronto

'Sculptura nella Citta', Public Squares, XXXVI Venice Biennale

1973 'Art in Space: Some Turning Points', Detroit Institute of Art 'Henry Moore to Gilbert and George: Modern British Art from the Tate Gallery', Palais des Beaux-Arts, Brussels

1974 'The Great Decade of American Abstraction: Modernist Art 1960 to 1970', Museum of Fine Arts, Houston

'Ten Years Ago . . . Painting and Sculpture from 1964', David Mirvish Gallery, Toronto

'Newport Monumenta', Biennial exhibition of outdoor sculpture, Newport, Rhode Island

'Sculpture in Steel', organised by Edmonton Art Gallery, Edmonton, Alberta; shown at David Mirvish Gallery, Toronto

1976 Galerie Ulysses, Vienna

'New Works in Clay', Everson Museum of Art, Syracuse

'English Art Today 1960–1976', The British Council, Commune di Milano, Palazzo Reale, Milan

'Painting and Sculpture Today 1976', Indianapolis Museum of Art

1977 'Silver Jubilee Exhibition of Contemporary British Sculpture', Battersea Park, London

Hayward Gallery, London, Arts Council of Great Britain

Biennale de Paris: 1959–1967, Paris

1978 '15 Sculptors in Steel Around Bennington, 1963–1978', Park-McCullough House Association, North Bennington, Vermont

'Late Twentieth Century Art', Sidney and Frances Lewis Foundation, National Tour of 18 museums 1978–1983

1979 'A Century of Ceramics in the United States, 1878–1978', Everson Museum of Art, Syracuse; also shown at Renwick Gallery of the National Collection of Fine Arts, Smithsonian Institution, Washington DC and Cooper-Hewitt Museum, New York

'Works of the Early '60s', Knoedler Gallery, London

'Corners: Painterly and Sculptural Work', Hayden Gallery, Massachusetts Institute of Technology, Cambridge, Massachusetts

1980 'J. Gonzalez, D. Smith, A. Caro, T. Scott, M. Steiner', Galerie de France, Paris and tour to Kunsthalle Bielefeld, Bielefeld; Haus am Waldsee, Berlin; Kunsthalle Tübingen, Tübingen

Galerie Wentzel, Hamburg

Knoedler Gallery, London

'L'Amérique aux Indépendants', 91e Exposition, Société des Artistes, Grand Palais, Paris

'Hayward Annual', Hayward Gallery, London

1981 'Groups IV', Waddington Galleries, London

1982 'A Private Vision: Contemporary Arts from the Graham Gund Collection', Museum of Fine Arts, Boston

'Casting: A Survey of Cast Metal Sculptures in the 80s', Fuller Goldeen Gallery, San Francisco

'Paper Sculpture', Harcus Krakow Gallery, Boston

'New Small Sculpture', Edmonton Art Gallery, Edmonton, Alberta

'Aspects of British Art Today', Tokyo Metropolitan Art Museum, and tour of five museums in Japan organised by The British Council

1983 'Aspects of British Art', Solomon R Guggenheim Museum, New York

'Britain Salutes New York' (Caro, Hockney, Nicholson), André Emmerich Gallery, New York

1984 'Six in Bronze', Williams College Museum of Art, Williamstown, Massachusetts; also shown at Museum of Art, Carnegie Institute, Pittsburgh; Columbus Museum of Art, Columbus, Ohio; Brooklyn Museum, New York

'The British Art Show', touring exhibition organised by The Arts Council of Great Britain

'Direction in Contemporary American Ceramics', Museum of Fine Arts, Boston

'Three Exhibitions about Sculpture III – Mind Over Matter', touring exhibition organised by The Arts Council of Great Britain travelling to Southampton, Bradford, Stoke-on-Trent and Sheffield

1985 'Transformations in Sculpture: Four Decades of American and European Art', Solomon R Guggenheim Museum, New York

'Human Interest', Cornerhouse, Manchester

1986 XLII Venice Biennale

'What is Modern Sculpture?', Centre Georges Pompidou, Paris

'Between Object and Image', touring exhibition Bilbao, Barcelona, Madrid

'Forty Years of Modern Art', Tate Gallery, London

Triangle Artists Show, Smith's Gallery, London

Adelaide Festival, Adelaide, Australia

Group Retrospective, Castlefield Gallery, Manchester

'Homage to Joan Miro', Joan Miro Foundation, Barcelona

'Thanks for the Memories', Harcus Gallery, Boston

Ceramic Workshop Experiments, travelling exhibition in US, organised by Brattleboro Museum, Vermont

'A Dozen Views on Paper', touring exhibition organised by the Cirencester Workshops for the Arts, Cirencester

'1st Biennale of Paper Art', Leopold Hoesch Museum, Düren, Germany

'British Sculpture from the 1950s and early 60s', New Art Centre, London

'Sculpture and Architecture – Restoring the Partnership', touring exhibition organised by the Welsh Sculpture Trust

'From Figuration to Abstraction', group exhibition, Juda Rowan Gallery, London

'Modern English Sculpture: Aspects of Modern English Sculpture', Lloyd Bregman Fine Art Ltd, Toronto, Canada

1987 'British Art in the 20th Century: The Modern Movement', Royal Academy, London, and Staats-galerie, Stuttgart

'Current Affairs: British Painting and Sculpture in the 1980s' Museum of Modern Art, Oxford, then touring: Hungary, Poland, Czechoslovakia (organised by The British Council). The Mucsarnok, Budapest; The National Gallery, Prague; The Zacheta, Warsaw

'Eisen Iron Fer', Hachmeister, Munster

'Ten British Masters', Arnold Herstand Gallery, New York

Gallery Artists show, Elizabeth Franck Gallery, Belgium

'The Self Portrait: A Modern View', touring exhibition organised by Artsite Gallery, Bath International Festival

'Nine British Artists', Francis Graham-Dixon Gallery, London

'The British Masters', Arnold Herstand Gallery, New York

1988 XLIII Venice Biennale

'Made to Measure', Kettle's Yard, Cambridge

Gallery Exhibition, Warwick Arts Trust

Tate Gallery Collection, Tate of the North, Liverpool

'Britannica, 30 Ans de Sculpture', Musée d'Evreaux, France; Museum Van Hedendaagse Kunst Antwerpen, Belgium

1989 Biennale de Sculpture Monte-Carlo '89

'From Picasso to Abstraction', Annely Juda Fine Art, London

First International Festival of Ironwork (F.I.F.I.)

'British Forged Metal Sculpture', Cardiff

1990 'Glasgow's Great British Art Exhibition', Glasgow Museums and Art Galleries

'Twenty One Years of Contemporary Art 1969–1990', The Compass Contribution, Glasgow

Fourth Australian Sculpture Triennial, National Gallery of Victoria 'Chagall to Kitaj' – Jewish Experience in 20th Century Art, Barbican, London

'Small is Beautiful', Flowers East, London

1991 'Art for the Land', Five Points Gallery, New York

'Not Pop – what the others were doing', Bernard Jacobson Gallery

'The 7th Henry Moore Grand Prize Exhibition', The Utsukushi-ga-hara Open Air Museum, Japan

'Sculpture & Sculptor's Drawings', William Jackson Gallery, London

1993 'Making a Mark', The Mall Galleries, London

'The Sixties', Barbican Art Gallery, London

'Here and Now', Serpentine Gallery, London

'Partners', Annely Juda Fine Art, London

'Images of Christ', St Paul's Cathedral, London

1994 'Tenth Anniversary', Castlefield Gallery, Manchester

Caro/Noland/Olitski: Symposium and Exhibition, Hartford Art School, University of Hartford, Connecticut, USA

Johnson Atelier, USA

Naumkeag Exhibition, Massachusetts

'Sculpture at Goodwood', Goodwood Sculpture Foundation UK

1995 'Cabinet Art', Jason & Rhodes Gallery

'British Abstract Art Part 2: Sculpture', Flowers East, London

1996 'Caro and Olitski: Masters of Abstraction Draw the Figure', New York Studio School of Drawing, Painting and Sculpture

'Un Siècle de Sculpture Anglaise' Galerie Nationale du Jeu de Paume, Paris

Museum Würth, Künzelsau, Germany

1997 'Grounds For Sculpture', Hamilton, New Jersey

'Abakanowicz, Bourgeois, Caro', Marlborough Chelsea, New York

1998 'British Figurative Art, Part 2: Sculpture', Flowers East, London

'Anthony Caro and Charles Ray', Greengrassi Gallery, London

'Fifty Years of Sculpture', Lothbury Gallery, NatWest Group, London

1999 'Shining Moment', Ameringer Howard Gallery, New York

Published 1999 by Museum Würth
and Verlag Paul Swiridoff, Künzelsau
© All rights reserved
ISBN 3 934350 01 1

Edited by Ian Barker
Designed and typeset in Trump by Dalrymple
Printed by BAS Printers Ltd

Photographic Credits:
numbers refer to illustration numbers
AKG Photo / © Succession Picasso / DACS 1999: 9
AKG London / Erich Lessing: 1
Shigeo Anzai: 4, 19, 21, 22, 34, p.55
Bridgeman Art Library, London / New York: 8, 15
David Buckland: 2, 11, 12, 13, 14, p.6
Carandente Archives: 33
Susan Crowe: 6
Volker Döhne: 31
André Emmerich: p.53
Fine Art Photographic Library Ltd / Yale / Artephot / Held: 10
Robert Freeman: p.49
Mick Hales: cover
Galerie Lelong, Paris: 3
Ugo Mulas: 18, 27
Courtesy Regen Projects, Los Angeles: 30
John Riddy: 5, 16, 23, 24, 32, 35, 36, p.54
Christopher Ward-Jones: 25
John Webb: 20
Museum Würth: p.4
Yorkshire Sculpture Park: 7